IMAGINARY ROYALTY

D1568869

Also by Miranda Field

Swallow

IMAGINARY ROYALTY

Miranda Field

Four Way Books
Tribeca

Copyright © 2017 by Miranda Field

No part of this book may be used or reproduced in any manner
without written permission except in the case of brief quotations
embodied in critical articles and reviews.

Please direct all inquiries to:
Editorial Office
Four Way Books
POB 535, Village Station
New York, NY 10014
www.fourwaybooks.com

Library of Congress Cataloging-in-Publication Data

Names: Field, Miranda, author.
Title: Imaginary royalty / Miranda Field.
Description: New York, NY : Four Way Books, [2017]
Identifiers: LCCN 2017000677 | ISBN 9781945588013 (pbk. : alk. paper)
Classification: LCC PS3606.I34 A6 2017 | DDC 811/.6--dc23
LC record available at https://lccn.loc.gov/2017000677

This book is manufactured in the United States of America and printed on acid-free paper.

Four Way Books is a not-for-profit literary press. We are grateful for the assistance
we receive from individual donors, public arts agencies, and private foundations.

This publication is made possible with public funds from the New York State Council on the Arts,
a state agency.

We are a proud member of the Community of Literary Magazines and Presses.

Distributed by University Press of New England
One Court Street, Lebanon, NH 03766

For Tom, Will, & Finn—
My family. You are everything to me.

& for my parents & sisters—
original ground of my life.

& in memory of Adam Sebastian Field-Angel.
Our love for you is indescribable.

Contents

Notes

1.

Winterreise

Hoarfrost forms on her limbs.
If we leave her here with birds and clouds
oscillating though her eyes, we fear
she'll wander. We risk losing her to conifers
and mosses. If you were raised by wild reindeer
could you be domesticated? We never were
able to tether her. If winter—
then wander.

Noblesse

When we were consanguine, the three
and I slept stacked on shelves, hieratic. Then

through the days we rode one another,
some tall in the saddle, some bridled, down

on all fours. Might one well-appointed female
stallion surmount her rider? Sisters, remember?

We tried. Each wore the bit, each tried to picture
her challenger in Ladybird underwear.

We experimented. I held the crop. You held it.
She did. She did. We took turns, or we

snatched. All pivoted on complex imperceptible, cyclical
exchanges, a sending sister's bio-chemical message

tempering the tenor of a receiving sister's behavior.
An act of blood, not something you acquire.

World Without End

Mama stops singing, stripped of high and low notes,
robbed of song cycles. She stopped stitching rows of ducklings
on smocked dresses aeons ago. Mama makes a pot of tea, says
Now the doctors have got me on this Dom Perignon! Paterfamilias
makes his lapdog velcro bat ears. He reads whole chapters
from his paperback about the Cambridge Five aloud.
Kim Philby, Burgess and MacLean, Blunt and Mystery Man,
like Flower Fairies they loitered in our childhoods.
We're grown, we don't misread ironic gestures, scatter toys.
We share prescriptions. Mama aerates the tea, tips the spout
half a foot above the cups. She pesters, Who wants milk? Who
sugar? Tea for nine. It slips her mind, how many times
the midwife visited. She scatters our names to the four corners.
Hard to distinguish one from another. Continuous silver
threads connect our tangled crowns.

Providence

The father who sired our father kept climbing, till he took
a tumble from the ladder. He thought this irrefutable, more so
than medical or divine opinion. He lay there listening

to leaves, which rustled like starched petticoats. Detaching,
his spirit gained energy, went scrambling up rungs
like an automaton, a ground-dweller taken over by a parasite
in the brain, saying climb, climb. Work faster, be fiercer

than before. *Hold this*, he instructed. The orchard invisible
in hospital light, still subject to laws of mechanics, branches kept
springing back. He wanted one more magnificent apple, one
deep in ghost-foliage. He'd gathered pails full, too many

to eat or give away. When he was done, he would commence
the simple process of turning to dust. He would see his phantom
harvest worm-consumed, even before his assistants pulled the blinds.

London Zoo, 1967

The animals in the zoo are all emotionally
labile multiple personalities. They stare at us,
they frown and laugh and bite, they mate and eat
and scream and improvise. In the chimp cage
big sister gathers rats' nests of little sister's chest hair
and yanks till little sister yanks back, a rat's
nest of big sister's chest hair. They lock like that.
You couldn't tear or cut or coax or saw them apart.
We feel that moment when roots, ripped out,
declare who's conqueror, our King Cones melt,
it's sunny. Here we are, where we're invited
to stare. Rabble: we're restless, hungry, critical,
entertained. The chimpanzees sit down to tea.

Superimpose

Another night done, another abrupt
vanishment of a parallel universe. I was sweeping

the catacombs, then on my knees scrubbing
an earth-brown bathtub ring. What does it mean,

the work assigned us in dreams? Uncompensated, desultory
management of messy existence, also the birthing

of non-human animals from time to time, the frequent
conspicuous naked bleeding in the schoolyard.

Come morning, my stomach feels like a metal bucket
with a mildewed sponge in it. I think a medication's fine-

tuning's in order. I'd make a note of it, only
your Western Philosophy lies

spine-up where I write. I hate to move it aside
for my Dictionary of Superstitions.

Molecule by Molecule

Why should I resume in dreams the childhood I've sloughed off incomplete? I speak from a center of a nebula of sisters, though only the cat's home with me, and she's hypnotized, she drags her silk length through the weeds in their jam jar till the weeds reach weed heaven, the silk silk heaven. In last night's dream my sisters and I keep shrieking, *There's too much fish sauce in it!* So effervescent we become when someone feeds us, we feel the need to complain and bicker—a reflex like blinking or folding wings, like engaging spinnerets. We're restless. The garden's unfolding, in every early bud an earwig waking up. The cat chirrups, a spring ecstatic, with snow crystals still clinging. I shrink to mother's child in my sleep, forget my children's mother.

Ha-ha Wall

After a seamless-seeming endlessness

an ineffable edge steps in,
protects against a too-much-with-us world
of work, weather, money, guns, grief, deception,
desire, etc. Let's laugh out loud here

all wet and shattered. Pity the collapsing
colony, the fox-wedding weather

keeping everyone in.
Everyone playing. We're such a bright
and shiny barrel of red monkeys,
a plastic anarchy.

Three-six-nine, we all drink wine,
the monkey chews tobacco on the telegraph line,
the line breaks the monkey gets choked
we all go to heaven in a little green boat.

Clap hands.

2.

Seven Times to Break & Mend

1.

I was partial. We touched to fibrillate. And each exists, each breathes
the other's name in secret. Coney Island's Pantone glitter-dusk. We
inverted—Cyclone, Cyclone, Wonder Wheel. Split a Corona, split another,

brushed arms, feigned nonchalance, grazed thighs, saw freak show artists
swallow glass, swallow swords, lip-synch Madonna wrapped in boa
constrictor coils. Bewitched, stricken with unconscious elective mutism,

we never said. Never touched. But nearly, at the aquarium—& nearly, too near
our jealous master's bedroom door—but not. Back at the squat, our sultan
began his petulant door-slamming. You talked my clothes off, T, just

once: ten below in your studio, I caught us in the angled mirror, your
breath-fog, my arm-clamped breasts. Your flash. I retracted. You played
with your lenses. Like Snake Lady, I was wearing a living

yoke. Even heavier. And hiding inside it. Plus I was married
to a marsh light. Enfleshed souls—can such contraptions levitate?

2.

Can such contraptions levitate? You eclipsed me, B, cowed me
with your look, pinned me to the couch in the dark. Now, with basic
formal constraints, I revisit your strength, the force of your crowbar

knee between my thighs. As instructed, I asked, *Please may I get up?*
You slapped back, *bitch can't take a bloody joke.* I was fourteen, the pinstriped
abortion-maestro, gloveless hands on my blue-veined swollen breasts,

leveled me, spat-out: *trollop* . . . This isn't the eighteenth century, "trollop"
an obsolete word. I no prostitute, he not Lord of me, this being the so-called
Land of the Free. Why I'm revisiting this travesty: your recent shitty

friend request. I would rather hit play-play-play again & again on little
boys kicking alley cats in repeating loops, than hit *accept.* I've been saying
Poetry's not therapy so long, I choke on my words. I should take it back:

isn't a kevlar-clad heart anti-art also? You replaced my subtle body
with your solidity. I may have taken my own medicine too faithfully.

3.

I may have taken my own medicine too faithfully, I thought: bite
your lip. I should have bent your will back with my own, K, but only
whimpered a question: *can't we wait?* Bic lighters, Benson & Hedges,

hot asphalt, peppermint rock, your grease-monkey hand steered
my black-nail-polished fingers to your clunky buckle. Your playground
grin didn't compute. Your eyelashes, floppy hair, boy-smell, orphan-

hood, I had no immune system. I was barely born. You pressed,
baited, lobbied hard, delivered a plush monkey hugging a felt heart,
tucked a condom in my breast pocket, followed me everywhere, upstairs

at parties, slithered your tongue past my teeth, stroked me, made me
all but come. You lavished much saliva and Motown on me, my body-
clock sped up. You were so sweet when I bled like a stuck pig

all over your Star Wars sheets. In case you're interested, I'm scribbling
abject apologies in a thought-bubble over your head. And I guess I accept.

4.

And I guess I accept, you fed me, P, you spooned bone broth
into my since-birth hungry mouth and it was critical, I couldn't
just be nourished. I paid you: all my attention, a moratorium

on outside friends. I dropped classes, stopped reading, spent hours
on the futon with you, staring at the ceiling fan, the split and scattered
light. My neophyte pleasure, your dreamy commentary, our

spangled, psychedelic nights. You lip-synched to Billie Holiday singing
Stormy Monday—lothario! You fed me shrimp paste on sugar cane, salt-
plums, starfruit in syrup. To cinch it: sticky green Sativa, your sociable,

attention-seeking cock. You more than fed, you impregnated me
with your ontology, I grew fat on it. Okay, maybe my body began its
literal dwindling, my voice grew thinner and higher, like the one gnat

you said you left an arm bare for, but my soul engorged. My soul
felt like a full moon when you left. But it was a new moon.

5.

A new moon, you, a mere slip, J, I almost forgot. I reduced a fillip
to a wisp, to avenge my even less substantial self, flipped the game,
released my powers. Used you to prove me. Not a matter of natural

animal instinct exactly. I saw you, and thought, Boy: You are huge,
golden, blue-eyed, born in an orange grove, beautiful with light
all around you, the face of an archangel, but next to mine, your spirit's

a puking, mewling baby. I'll bend you in two. You may have been born
with a lacrosse stick over your shoulder, but beside my history, yours
is as tiny and protected as a caged thing's, as easily controllable, as

lightly crushed under the right conditions. . . . I snatched you, gratuitously,
shoved you in the shower stall, yanked your drunk blonde head back by its
ringlets, made you mine. Then when you woke and adored me faithfully

all puppy-eyed next day, I wanted to bury you. I'd invaded, I'd occupied
like an enemy. (I confess, in a bloody sonnet sequence, ceremonious.)

6.

A bloody sequence, ceremonious—in 1685: *the face of the dead burgomaster whose wolfish habits and disposition in life had terrorized women was strapped to a live wolf's head, whose snout had been cut off, whose body in a tight suit*

of flesh-coloured cere-cloth, and adorned with a chestnut brown wig, was then hanged by order of the court to atone. . . . A non-human with no criminal mind punished for a man's crimes! In an about-face, now men who perpetrate

rape are "animals." What if, shape-shifting stranger, I went downtown, re-sketched your visage to make it more wolflike? Then would several dozen women shrug off amnesia, wake up, identify the perpetrator of our grievous

harms, our vehicular abductions? With bared fangs, foaming, scarlet, rank saliva—that's right, I've inserted you into a children's story, cross-dressed. . . . Years pass, some vicious moves I learned in city-funded self-

defense have stuck, some haven't. Some exceed me. I could cut off a stray dog's snout or tail as easily as jam my fingers deep in a man's eye sockets.

7.
(for Tom)

Deep in a man's eye sockets, to make a home? To find a stopping place
for the endlessly vagrant self. To be ignited, to finish heated, interlocking,
hardly-ambulatory organisms with lateral taproots spliced. We think, ah,

lucky us, then await disaster, which doesn't and doesn't happen. Like a series
of tests, we touch the same flesh over and over, hope the data gained remains
mysterious. Releases us. From loneliness? Desire? To touch another

triggers exchanges: elide dividing spaces, and intermingle at the cellular
level. Falling in love with you was spiral-pathed, all ensuing moments
meant falling so far, so slowly, I might extend a hand, pluck a book

from a shelf: *Theory of Epidemiological Drift.* Lying on leaves, staring up
through branches, sharing eyes, on a single afternoon we encounter maybe
a trillion microbes; some respond by changing. Like mirrored surfaces

in public places, we contain strangers. You half are, and half aren't. We both
are partial. We touch and fibrillate. And each exists, each breathes.

Formal Photo at Dusk on Adirondack Chapel Steps

A back brace for the mother.
A ghillie suit of roses, awkwardly fitted, for the father.
Sporrans of cut sod for the interlopers, the appended men.
The bridesmaids' French braids wreathed with grass snakes.
The bride's black hair waiting to fade-out to white.
Squirrels enough to stain and eat through folds of silk in storage.
Jays to eat the rice grains from the grass.
Crows for the roast. Worm casts.
The groom's feelings floating faraway, *New Jersey, New Jersey.*
Later, a rose-tinged supermoon.

The Proust School of Impermanence

Enrolled again, against your wishes,
watched, lest you escape. Your grandest
echo-chamber's inmost inmate, muted.
Can't eat, can't stop the thought-stream's
slow leaking away. Can't say what life form
you're extracted from, if grown in full
moon, or sun, or utter dark. If you possess
true limbs with nerve-ends. So then
write a book of every thing: of when, and how,
and what can be deciphered by an *I*
unverified. You have bioluminescence, India ink,
rice paper, a blanket-tent. Let it rain.

Of Stature

Special corridors exist for the to-be-written-
off, as for the hurriedly-whisked-away; midget hatches
for obsolete child-size chairs; double-hinged cat
doors, slave quarter Dutch doors narrower

even than a mouse's or Death's. Also gates
an accent closes or opens. In the elevator, Eleni,
graciously: "Have I introduced my *aspen*?"
Meaning she'd married him, and like a ship mast's

shadow flung on a forest floor at sunup,
he suddenly stretched; or is it that we women
telescope? When the doors opened, he had to stoop

to go through, and I was awed by her because
she'd grown him from nothing. I felt my own
woods whiten, my aspens stake the four directions.

Art Is Long as an Elephant Chain

To make extra rent, I take seasonal work staging
a magnificent media event, I wave a Ringling Brothers
bull-hook with one hand and manage traffic with the other.
My herd plods passively in a chain, similarly my heart
is linked to doggedness by contract. The tunnel takes us
under the East River, through entry, blindness, forbearance,
long-suffering, to gridlock, sirens. A gaseous sunrise
strikes their sequined headdresses, then a light-
as-spring-rain applause. Do they feel greeted? What is it
applause brings to the tunnel? Attachment is intrinsic
to an elephant's emotional repertoire, an all-consuming, lovesick
filial piety, and, undeniably, grief. Can a heart weighing forty
to sixty kilos know lightness though? It gets less and less
simple going home after work to wrangle my language.

Strength Card (Fortitude VIII)

Fortitude clamps the jaws of the lion
with tightrope walker composure. My major
Arcana arranged, my future unlike my past
will be a simple-syrup domestic dream,
my children will dance with arms entwined
by a placid lake. Would I sell this future
for a quarter of whatever the lion-jaw-holder
is on? I wonder. To be of the type open
to the company of carnivores, to be licked
lovingly, like warm ganache from a generous-size
spoon. In fact, I have been the recipient of
such attentions and it wasn't enough. To lie down
with the lion, to feel no need to explain my
exhaustion, even the garlands of nightshade
encircling him twice, tied to me. This might be
emblematic of enduring married happiness.

Whoso List

In the middle of a meeting I excuse myself, and all down silent polished halls feel the dog breath on my slingback heels. In plaid some hunters roam, in suits of grey and slate and stone, and all as weary as I of the hunt's form. I come here to wash hands, I come here to take time, though time's too subtle to be taken by a slacker. I hear horns, hooves, hounds. I hear them near, I hear them far and fading out. Faithfully reflected, bleached by fluorescent light, I look a gutted thing, and skinned, my makeup gone, my clothes a net of wind. I say to her who hangs, maturing, in the mirror, well. We were a-hunted once. Some arrowy afterthoughts still dangle in wind, but clearly the hunters have galloped on. Where now to run, and from whom?

Cybele

I blushed—it was rush hour,
we walked down Broadway,
she demonstrated on her own large breasts
how the metal plugs latched on,
a little roughly, but not so sudden
as to frighten the cow and stop the milk.
The apparatus unequivocal,
the sucking rhythmic, mechanical.
This is how it's actually done
on misty farms, in agricultural zones.
I come from a city. A novel taught me
how to make an udder flow:
form an okay sign with finger and thumb,
soften the o's rigid rim, enclose
the teat and tug, as on a bell pull, or
school-girl's pigtail. And know
you must be on your knees, you must not be
machine, you must be close to straw
and creaturely.

Spirit vs. Matter

Winter takes us just as Earth's axis
tilts away from the sun.

Nature breaks down her materials
to constituent chemicals, chemicals to molecules,
molecules to atomic particles, then energy

is released. On small islands, the topography's altered
by entropy. In every parish, churchyards
grow overloaded, swollen, churches appear to have

sunk. Some lost parishioner or other
is always scratching to be let in or out, whimpering.
There's something moving around under the snow.

If you put your ear to the underworld, you can track
the tunneling of star-nosed moles.

Nautilus

There's this transparent shell around us.
Water resistant, airtight, soundproof, fireproof.
Tonight, in this heavy rain, we could perhaps go out.
Should we go out tonight? We think the same.
Only if it's not raining too hard, you say,
as if rain were radioactive. I am suddenly uneasy
about the snugness of our his-n-hers shell.
On rainy nights, on nights when palmetto bugs levitate,
we could drift down the elevator shaft and through the city
risking nothing. Ambulances would float past,
delivery bikes would peddle silently against traffic.
Among throngs but not of them, O, mirror neurons. . . .
Even on the subway on a Saturday night
nothing would bump into us. We would bump into only
one another. The city has an End Times energy.
The die-in at Grand Central, the candles and carnations.
You and I could float over there, place a flower, find a place
in the potter's field with all the others. Our shell filters
the air. It is temperate, we're obscenely safe.

3.

I simply cannot see where there is to get to.

A Soul So Watched

Lights off, windows black mirrors. No paths, no trees, no other houses. We slump together in the dark, we have clambered over one another into an alcove of shadow cut in the snow. The snow blows sideways around our black mirror-box. We crawl on all fours under the dog's blanket and dissolve. We make spittle and snot; strands of each sister's hair stick to the faces of the others. We contract, a Gordian knot of spines and arms, distinction lost in an animal contortion, and you can hear at our center, from somewhere inside her, the reverse birth-moan. None of us is her own grown self now. Reconjoined, four sisters. The magnetic pull is awful, gravity unbearable, and, oh our bodies are staved. It is the center we seize around, the sister in whom the hole has opened. The cold blows through us all.

*

Drifts deepen behind black glass.

After sleep suffocates, the fact swings back again. Understanding
slams. Induces vomiting.

The milky, endless swirling seems a pre-apocalyptic lyric
dream. As poison mushrooms

mimic benign, the neighbor's Christmas lights blink
wickedly. We're trying to swallow

an assassination.

*

Online communities discuss a common grief-phenomenon, the "visitation dream." An indication that a visitation has "actually occurred" is how everything in a visitation dream seems "too real to not be him."

The first night, he reached his sister on her cell. His voice. He said, *No worries, Em, I'm just stuck in Central Islip. . . .*

It was weeks before he came to me. His five-year-old self, Superman tights bagging around his ankles. He came running from the garden, buried his head in my body. Wanted his hurt head kissed. *Poor head, poor head,* I said. *I feel it*—under the hot, sweaty cornsilk—*a huge goose egg!* His beautiful head. It was perfect.

More often than you'd think, the dead and grieving reconnect by phone. The phone rings in the dream, but commonly the room where the ringing comes from is too far away to reach in time. Or the ringing comes from behind a wall, or locked door. Or the room where the ringing comes from is dark, or on fire, or under water, or boarded over.

But if you are able to answer, you want to keep dreaming, to keep the line open. But you know you will wake up, and waking, break the connection.

*

Another form of visitation happens when you're wide awake: the lost appear in alternate forms—in our gardens, our kitchens, in the woods where we walk. An unusually large moth on the wall; a strange dog sitting in the yard for hours; a wasp caught between panes of glass— they are real, but we project upon them grief-symptoms.

In Central Park, on my way to work, a squirrel seemed to be following me, and each time I stopped, it stopped, it looked at me, as if it wanted to say . . .

But having so mastered the self, to come back timid, twitchy?

*

The more real body hidden inside the body that walks around, that everyone sees, has suffered a massive blunt trauma. The sternum feels it, the chest cavity constricts. The heart we say is broken, registers the impact: there's a sunken, bruised sensation under the breastbone. The heart, blindsided, stunned, needs urgent care, but instinctively eats dirt. Rejects sympathy, sews a nettle shirt in secret. Wants to be cut out. Begs to be buried.

But it isn't *us* he conceived this for. The terrible plan, then the level-headedness with which he saw it through, detail by detail— belongings sorted, boxed up, donated, given away. The small apartment's jammed, closets emptied. Every sock, key, cup, jar, pen; every thumbtack: gone. Fridge cleaned, windows, walls stripped bare.

But the note, tossed-off, ad-hoc:

> *If I am* [don't write it] *when you find me,*
> *I apologize* [it's unbearable] *for the inconvenience* . . . .

And for us—no, not possible—informed over the phone—what to do now with the details? Method: most alien. Most violent. Means: *overkill,* the cop said. A 45. Favorite of self-annihilators. So common in these cases, cops call it *The Judge*.

Somehow he was found (when? how? by whom?), among abandoned, jumbled headstones. The few things in his jeans pockets: "not suitable for viewing." The note, folded quick, stuffed deep down, ditto: An apology. To whom, we will never know. To the stranger who found him—forgive me—

I dedicate this page.

*

A missing swath of time, blizzard, FedEx truck stuck in drifts. An engine
    idling.
Knock at the door, a clipboard and pen, a package, and the howling

storm, and the sobbing, the unacceptable, inhuman contents of the box
confirmed, signed for, accepted. The piano-room. Unheated room disused

filled with rotting, forgotten things. Where the piano warps, the shell
    chair's springs
burst out, the rolled-up dog-stained rugs rot to dust: here we hide this
    from her.

After the room is reassigned, the flow of Chopin from the body of the
    Beckstein,
out the door, into the hallway, up the stairs, through the ceilings, ends.

*

Sound of hot words
by the door
to the room where the ashes wait—
someone breaks down,
lashes out.

One sister only
chosen to stand with his mother
at high tide, others wait home
wondering: Is it done?
Is he gone?

The dogs bark, anxious.
Sobbing, anger
in the room with the box.
worldpain—

what the box contains
(I apologize
for writing this)
shifting in the box
when we hold it in our arms.

Not dust. Nothing

the wind could lift,
disperse through air over water.
Like sand and grit mixed
with crushed rocks,

what shuts us up: Demolition.
Moraine. It contains
such a weight of shame.

Flesh of her flesh, placed between
a vase of flowers and a photo—
black frame, 8 x 10—on the piano.
She couldn't look. Memorialized,
a newborn: his red face, mittened
fists raised to screwed-tight eyes.
In his hospital-issue striped stocking
cap. Infants come too small for clothing
but are quickly covered: The sky-blue
organic cotton onesie with white batik
clouds, feet, snaps, it was my baby-
shower gift, we bought it that fall day
on Atlantic Avenue. Beside the birth-
stunned baby, the almost-man's ashes,
his grown body rendered down near
exactly to his birth weight. In an over-
sized Nesquik box. We'd said yes
to an "upgrade," zombified, in shock.
We ordered over the phone: an upgrade:
"basic box" to (least expensive) "urn."
What came was an oblong, cardboard,
weirdly tall, box-dressed-as-urn, meaning
wrapped in glossy craft-paper. It jolted:
Mirroring—*exactly*—the sky-blue-
with-clouds clothing she'd chosen
to bring him home in. On the urn/box, stock
photography. The stupid, "meaningful" gesture
from the funeral home's kitschy, maudlin
imagination: across the dreamy heaven-

blue paper, in a puffy font, white,
like skywriting, photoshop ectoplasm:
Going Home . . . It shook and shut us up.
He was newborn when the photo was taken.
Her body had been his only home.

*

When it is suddenly, impossibly soon, time to stage a show—to make like we can let him go—you'd think we were relinquishing him just weaned. We conjure up mists-of-time versions of him for his twenty-something friends, they have driven here through a blizzard from Oregon. We share his famous-in-the-family pee-on-the-ceiling feat, his beautiful *putto*-belly, his early speech habits: "fowlers" for flowers. Bullied, sullen, beautiful, small-of-stature. Untamable, oppositional cynic, adolescent ironist! He'd been my sister's "bump," undreamt, then bursting forth, an imp, a fussy fingerling on her breast, passed to my arms, to each auntie's in turn, in the milky, unreal minutes after birth. Firstborn to the falling-apart circle of sisters, it seemed he'd broken a spell: as if he'd cut the old, frayed cord attaching us to trauma and trouble.

*

Three peripheral mothers. Detritus
of the constellation farthest from the epicenter,
we manage, we pin-prick-pupil body-doubles,
we sweep, gather plates and glasses, pick up Kleenex,
petals, crackers, we rinse bottles. Clean-up crew
after a memorial, before which all were birthdays.
How many? How many clever sheet cakes
have we devised? To look like Pikachu, like Nemo,
like a fire truck. No ribboned balloons, no Mylar
hearts or mermaids. Still, scattered paper plates.
Two suns gone down in black glass, a haloed moon
dragged up. Chairs and rugs put back, candles
snuffed, lamps switched on. We sit on the floor
around her, the mute, the frightening fourth mother,
our sister, at the center, in her pain amazing.
Under the solar plexus, the heart's unsurvivable
injury radiates. It's massive, radioactive.
When a death is sudden, when it's violent, exponential
shock. Our chests take the impact. We've caved in.
Breathing can't obtain. Our spines, unsupportive,
wind round our souls like snakes. Then, miraculous,
white, pink, and multi-colored pharmaceuticals,
opioids, palliatives, passed palm to palm.

He is not in his room.
Not in the yard where the trampoline is a white mound.
The rosebushes disappear.
Whiteness heaped on whiteness.
Not in the high black branches, in the black between stars.
Not in the forgery of royalty
that is this universe.
Not communicating with us via kitchen lights' flickering.
When the lights flicker, it's the electrical grid under the pressure of the storm.
This whole world emptied of him.
No residue of sight inside the glasses we must file paperwork with the coroner's
    office to retrieve.
We might put them on and look: the wrong prescription. Speckled lenses.
Not the spring, fall, winter trees reflected in the school bus windows.
Not the skies, seasons, streets, strip malls.
Today it is raining, and amazing, and he's not anywhere.
Not in his room, the yard, the evening, the sound of wind in trees.
Not in any of the lame forgeries
that are the days, the hours, the minutes.
His thrift-shop jacket slung on a chairback, elbows bent, is empty.
He is not human-shaped shadow, not fiction, not ghost.
Not here, not real, not laughing, arguing, thinking, speaking, standing,
    sleeping.
This nothingness. It clings to everything.

*

The literature is large. You could read through the night all winter, all spring and not find an answer.

In language or in silent thought we must capture and express ourselves in relation to life and begin to come to our essential function: as shepherds of being.

His mother watched him, vigilant at a distance. His friends were aware.

Mitvelt: the world of interpersonal relation; Eigenvelt: the intrapsychic world; Umvelt: the world of nature: Survival depends on finding a home in at least one of these worlds, without which: unbearable psychache.

How does a soul so watched become so lost?

Prison may be considered an island of barbed wire, iron bars, and armed guards, surrounded by an ocean of time. The mental jail of psychache, although invisible, is harder. Its ceiling is too low for its occupant to stand tall, its walls too narrow to allow easy breathing, and the cell too short to stretch out.

Did he think of us? Under his sinking ceiling, as long as he allowed himself continuance, breathing there, as the room constricted, breathing, thinking.

There is nothing that can be written to explain; the coroner's report is useless. Even the note he neatly wrote said nothing. *If I am* [but how can he be?] *when you find me . . . .*

Went out of life and put a period to being.

*

And in the midst of our private disaster, vaguely, we're aware: an airplane disappears, and in the ballroom of a hotel in Beijing, family members, friends and girlfriends, mothers, sisters, neighbors wait.

What is this parallel news? It is a climate not requiring senses. A sky empty of radar and empty of weather. Or a sky from which weather has been washed away by a switched off transponder.

(And what is my sister? A nest of hair matted at the back where she lies in her bed and stares, like one searching skies. When you put your arms around her, she feels wooden. She doesn't know what she is, and she is not what we know.)

At the arrivals gate the mothers, sisters, brothers, uncles, aunts, beginning to feel the non-arrival, silent among themselves, not yet connected to these strangers, these mothers and fathers, sisters and brothers of strangers.

Why would square miles of ocean open and open, the possible point of impact widen and widen, the search area double in the space of one night? To accommodate an unthinkable number? So many on board, 239 "souls": an exponential expansion of "passenger list." The disappeared airplane had a destination it missed, it intentionally detoured from, it rejected.

We feel it: Blood begins to boil over in Beijing, the mothers have collapsed and been revived and collapsed again in the arms of the fathers and uncles and brothers who have sweated through everything they have with them. They begin to bombard with water bottles the bearers of no news. They need to point fingers. The mothers and brothers and

46

aunts and sisters, the fathers and uncles. They need to lash at the origin of devastation, not stare at blameless space.

Like weather conditions, like plankton passing through a net, anything installed dependably in the phenomenal world under one condition might vanish from the next. Someone says "searching for a needle in ten thousand haystacks, a pebble in an area the size of Russia . . . ." But they need it, they need the pin. They need the map, to be able to find on it some point in space, and stick it with the pin.

*

A flight recorder emits an ultrasonic beacon but in time it dies and we go blind, the reporter records the searchers saying. There is nothing to see, we hear only a beacon inside our heads, our blood, our dreams. Nothing speaks up.

It is hard to look at our own lost one in the photographs, the woozy pumpkin-head of a happy baby, a sleeping child, a painfully awkward ring-bearer, a baby-fatted boy avoiding the camera. As for the man the boy was close to becoming, we cannot see him, we must list the identifying tattoos on the left arm and upper back of the man he was at the moment he stopped.

At a distance, we give permission for the Judge to be judged, sentence the weapon, yes, destroy it, *we give you permission*. We give our permission, verbal then written, but still a letter comes, the medical examiner's office sends an official request on letterhead, it makes her get out of bed, pick up a pen.

And finally the papers to say: also eradicate his physical shape, his extension in space, the arms, the hands—they were smallish and seemed gentle—one steadied the other as it pulled the trigger. If it were possible for us to see, just one more time—but though we ache to hold him whole in our arms, who could forgive those hands?

We're left with boxes of pictures.

My own child's first birthday, his face completely eclipsed by a balloon on a ribbon.

Her child, baby whose birth made a corridor for us, sister after sister, rooms with the next and next and next birth-bed: his cheek sandy, the sunset in his eyes, he squints, his shoulders swamped by an uncle-shirt, the t-shirt comes down to his feet, like a toga; he stands, smiling up from the center of a starburst of strangers' footprints on an emptying trampled beach, summer, 1986.

On a bed, in a London flat, blue-grey northern light falling through a picture window, he is the first baby: he is a newborn, sleeping. The plush lambskin under him, it was handed down many times. My own child soothed by it, second-hand.

There is a sequence of bright green Easter scenes (silly ritual he always managed to avoid): we set up the same composition, after the egg hunt, year after year: All the cousins shoulder to shoulder, like the bars of a xylophone, side by side under a tree, youngest and tallest first, sun-struck heads descending in increments. The second-oldest cousin bookends all the others, except him. Oldest, smallest, missing.

There is never the wherewithal to sort the photos into albums. None of us ever managed to assemble albums, order the chaos. We rummage through the shoe-box of pictures together. So many glimpses—shot through with sun, under-exposed, messed up, thumbs blocking faces, sconces sprouting from heads like horns—

the haunted spaces and the apparitions, double-exposed. All the magical and abject, the misaligned and overlapping instants in which he lived with us persist, but he is gone from them. We can tear the pictures apart, we could frame them, surround them with flowers and candles, but his face has stilled, his body stopped. He is lost to our eyes.

(2/1/14)

4.

Arnica, Absolution, Ambien

No longer able to sleep "like a baby,"
to soothe myself I stare at the turbid-to-glassy lake
of my mind, I let rise to the surface anonymous
bodies, whose only steady work is painstakingly replacing
opacity with bioluminescence. I take an opiate, a sign
lights up—a soft, nostalgic V A C A N C Y in rain—
I take another, the sign flickers. Don't waste your breath
then asking who I am. Snagged on a twig in the woods
glowing translucent cocoon at sundown—
the least of its worries is the worm.

Spare Room

Fell asleep staring at an empty ant farm.

How we play with others, how we treat what we keep, if we bear
hunger in mind, if we answer when strays scratch at the door,
depends on the animals we kept—if we pulled wings off insects, if we
    tucked in mice
for the night, if we named, if we brushed, if we made four legs fit two-
sleeved dresses, if we offered plates for licking.

All the mute spirits of our creations and creatures, in what ways
have we sustained? Have we communicated across divides?

Woke up copying an ant farmer's awkward signature
over and over, all down the length of *The Dangerous Book for Boys.*
What we keep and what we let escape, the criteria change, what lives,
    what dies,
and how, and why, and what helpless things we carry, which
we'd be willing to mother forever. One couldn't need a room at a better
    time,
someone said, with one left vacant so lately.

Slept deeply, dreamed my sister, speechless,

lifted her sweater to show the place where all our lost creatures still
latch on. Are you eating, I asked her, is it sufficient?

Does it equal all the feeding?

Crib

Just learning to stand, I could grow dizzy. Holding the bars, my stance unstable, I follow the four shadows of my mobile's crows across the ceiling to where they snag in the lattice pattern of our magic lantern. Sometimes in my hypnogogic state, I see you cup the infant-sized mossy skull you found under our mother's dress one long, deep, moonless night before we made friends. I could have grown up and grown old watching you practice becoming my sister, scrubbing the cranium clean under the cold tap with bleach. I wake up when you whisper something through the bars. Whatever it is, it terrifies, and feels affectionate, and hurries my pulse.

True Crime

Restless in my haunted childhood, awake in my toddler bed, I dug at a gash in the rose-strewn wall until the gritty plaster was exposed, and a hole opened, matted with human hair. Each night I pulled the hairs from the wall, and the longer, the more knotted they were, the more morbid I grew. I grew into a bigger room. I got a lock on my door. When an immature creature reaches for the adult stage, her anxious queries and suspicions, they function as feelers. I felt my way from fairy tales to police procedurals. There were many x-ed out eyes on many hourglass figures, many x-ed out breasts, in many crawlspaces, in many vulture-grips. Under the floorboards of ordinary houses, under the home-spaces, as under the wild, as under the municipal, the mysteries. Small sounds seemed to be sending messages, doors slammed when no one was home, sash-cords snapped as if hungry to decapitate. A full moon meant mood swings, meant mania as much as search dogs tugging on leashes, leading to disturbed earth. Anxiety, suspicion, and the moon's influence—they have continued to keep me awake. It would be counter-instinctive to medicate. When the feelers fall asleep the remainder has to stay awake.

The Uninvited

Spirit Who Drags Things Backwards.
The Crone-like Knitting Ghost.
Drifting-off Ghost.
Protective Spirit In the Shape of a Lap Dog.
Plate-chipping Ghosts.
Spirit Who Divulges Details No One Should Know.
Wrong-blooded Spirit Who Sobs Too Loudly.
Apparition in the Shape Of a Man Having an Eye in the Place of His Anus.
Terrifying Tunnel Ghost Who Haunts the Long, Dark, Empty Birth Canal.
Spirit Who Speeds the Decay of Cut Flowers.
A Thorn-like Barb with a Loudly Beating Heart.
Ghost that Induces All Who Dwell Here to Eat Only Sweet Things
For the First Few Weeks.
Tree-spirits Who Cause the Ends of Twigs to Issue Forth Rotted Blossom.
Burning Wheel Spinning Faster and Faster with Old Polaroids at the Center.
Nausea Monster.
Ghost to Whom Words Won't Come, Phantom Who Stutters
No Words No Words, Over and Over.

The Spirits of Suicide Forest

Aokigahara, Japan

Yūrei, they loiter, they're lost, they lean on crooked pines.
Reported by day-trippers, their behavior ranges from polite to brusque
to pure absurdist theater, nihilist, or just prankish—
bottles taken from day packs stuck upside down in the mud, the braids
    of twin sisters tied together.
Some, who can blame them, rummage through the rotted belongings
littering the forest floor. One's tangled hair
has snagged on a branch, one's necktie's on backwards.
One's pills lie, scattered dice, on moss, and mints, makeup, cufflinks,
    pocket mirrors.
Some whom gravity perhaps dragged down too long seem to have come back
as butterflies or gnats, ants, ticks, no-see-ums, of negligible mass.
Visitors who witness these phenomena report feeling changed, challenged,
lost, reversed, x-rayed, undone.
Addled by shock or grief, unsure of what they've seen, some, who can
    blame them,
first blurt out then refuse to speak again of what they've seen.
Others report feeling the strangest unspoken communion, as one can
with a bedraggled stray animal. It's hungry. It haunts.
You know it belonged once, to someone.

Tilted Stones

Wild woods touch St. Mary's
churchyard here, here, does this
hurt? Dotted over with daisies,
primroses, moss pillows,
hillocks studded with china-
blue poison amonita caps.
We walk, we talk about God,
that ghost not there for me.
And the weather, and the last
clump of ancient Fulminating
Mandelbrot Archaebacteria
in a specimen jar in Germany.
It has expired. A pity! An
anachronism. We swing
the whinging iron gate. We're
tramping through mud. The birds
have returned. A miracle!
But real. We change subjects
every few steps. We wonder:
which genus is most Rapture-
ready? Flutelike? Expeditious?
Which will be the last to incubate
descendants? Children love robins
as much as chocolate. I drag my kids
up the exact hills I was dragged up.
Miserable, over stiles, through
swarms of midges, then ecstatic,

they plump up with oxygen, as does
the landscape. A charming dimple
becomes a wrinkle, ridge, cicatrice,
long barrow, stone circle, tarn.
I think, didn't a woman incubate
a duck's egg in the heat between
her breasts? Would it work if
one were tucked in a man's
armpit, if he stopped moving,
submitted to bed rest? I think
about bed rest. Honest work
in the copse. A murmur of thunder.
Twig-snaps, rustles in the branches,
A cloudburst, on then off. Then *Tea-
kettle-ettle-ettle* prattle everywhere.
Certain birds inherit all the genetic
instructions they need to sing
the family songs. Others not.
St. Mary's bells fill the woods
with magic, all at once repetitive
and wildly strange. An analog
and electric canticle. I ask my own
brain: since my musty encyclopedia
is growing old, my scrolls, my
Alexandria, when I'm finally,
as will happen, orphaned, what if
I still want to know things? What if
a fallen starling fledgling wakes

and thinks it's a wood thrush? What if
moths raised a magpie as their own?
We stand there, while nothing answers.
Then prattle bubbles up again.

On the Subway

Staring warily into a stranger's ear, after an era of only
my child's ear, this flowing out and in again is exponentially

strange. Storm drain poured-through, funnel-to-faraway.
The tunnel drips sounds. I know we've stopped. It's raining,

ropes of raindrops suspended from street level gratings, silver
lengths of chain, single links striking tracks, like a kindergarten

glockenspiel. In the dark, my need to get somewhere dims. A film
of swarming humming fills my head between stops. Din of residual

industries above? Tinny music's leaking, a stranger's ear-
buds spilling *tzchk-tzchk*. The stranger's newspaper:

breaking news: mass migrations, obliteration of whole
regions by apathy, by revolutions. I think I am beginning

maybe to understand (drowsily, my face now nearly close enough
to combine with my child's) how quick the numerous reversals

of power, capitals toppled, cities burned. Having stared so long
into this intimate space, I think, it's really time to go out—or is it?

What if I stare some more, what if I lean and lean, and linger, loiter,
if I create more caves to wander, more waxy, inner-lit lilies to slip into,

even smaller, deeper, narrower corridors. . . . If history continues
bypassing us, my child and me. . . . If our train stalled forever

under the East River . . . we'd think nothing. I and my love's
captive—as if stilled by volcanic ash—staring out, being staring into.

Vanitas

1.

Bird-babble
related to barometric

flip-flops
fills vase-shaped trees.

Eros arranges
encounters, cross-fosters

glossolalia,
green language.

Visible nature's
a moral multiverse. . . .

Harlot! Mascot! Harlot!
the dun-feathered & bright red ones

chitter. From certain
angles spiderwebs

appear: silver
and exact

in sunlight, and flitting minutia
trapped midair.

2.

Silk net with lead-weight load—

a luna,
or other behemoth—the highly elastic *I* distorts

to make space,
stretches, extends an open-ended invitation

mimicking the curvature of all space-time
illustrated digitally in the Hall of Natural History, a fractal

lattice, dilating exponentially, like God's reticello collar!

And if I can't receive the feeling-signals of all things I'm captive to
and captivate back, even so, briefly, sweetly even,

the machine breathes.

Why Ever Winter?

For the sawfly's cocoon
to freeze to a twig
in the woods, for the mourning
cloak butterfly to replenish
its energies in the supine
lengths of dead trees.
For these reasons
we have winter,
over and over. And over-
wintering which is how
some creatures pass through
killing frosts and starving times
while others' wings
hang tattered.
When summer ends
you could say the latter
adumbrate the "loveless dust,"
reduced to
near-negligible particles
of biological matter
clinging to
leaf-litter, or
you could stop
talking for half a minute.
Even mind-talk
makes a racket. Listen
to creation and creation's
children's creations:
dust and pollen

seeding clouds,
ice-crystals
spinning down
through bare trees,
glitter sprinkled
on skating scenes
across Advent calendars.

Pastoral

Then just the two of us alone at last, under a tree in Central Park in spring, on our backs in the grass, looking up. Our spirits had been injured. Winter was over. I don't think I can make it through another one, I said (another grief, another tundra?) to which he replied, something about my face, and feeling winter's wind. Then the tree stirred. All of creation (until we're sailing on a painted ship upon a painted ocean) is continually in motion. We were looking up together, my love of many jangling years and I, the two of us on our backs in the grass shared a single line of vision, still we reported to one another what we saw. From farther away the trees in the park made a continuous gently seething ocean surface; but to us, up close, each leaf moved in its own elliptical or spiral trickle or eddy of space: more like a loosely choreographed swirl of pixels or a star nursery than the to-and-fro sea. I was watching, I was drifting off, I wanted away, but I couldn't stop following the leaves whose flickers effleuraged my sleepy, slowly-closing eyes. It was a blissful, enmeshing feeling. As if hundreds of delirious kings and Tom O'Bedlams kept up their whispering near my head on a heath. *For the rain it raineth every day.*

Notes

"Winterreise"—The title (trs. Winter Journey) is a song cycle for voice and piano by Schubert. The question of wild vs. domestic in the poem comes from my reading of Piers Vitebsky's *The Reindeer People* (Houghton Mifflin, 2005). Reindeer are possibly the only animals in human history originally domesticated for the purpose of hunting their wild cousins. Modern wild reindeer cannot be domesticated. It is thought that today's wild reindeer is not the ancestor of its domestic counterpart, and that the wild strain that was domesticated no longer exists.

"Whoso List"—The title is from Sir Thomas Wyatt's sonnet to "Whoso List to Hunt, I Know Where is an Hind."

"Strength Card" is for Rebecca Kinzie Bastian, who read my cards one very dark afternoon, spinning her interpretations to make me feel all would one day be well again.

In "Seven Times to Break & Mend," which is a sort of nonce form crossed with a sonnet crown, in section 6, the italicized lines are (paraphrased) from *The Criminal Prosecution and Capital Punishment of Animals*, by E.P. Evans. This is the passage in full:

> In 1685, a were-wolf, supposed to be the incarnation of a deceased burgomaster of Ansbach, did much harm in the neighborhood of that city, preying upon the herds and even devouring women and children. With great difficulty, the ravenous beast was finally killed; its carcass was then clad in a tight suit of flesh-coloured cere-cloth, resembling in tint the human skin, and adorned with a chestnut brown wig and a long whitish beard; the snout of the beast was cut off and a mask of the burgomaster's features substituted for it, and the counterfeit presentment thus produced was hanged by order of the court.

"Cybele"—The title refers to the ancient Anatolian Earth-Goddess, often depicted in art with numerous pairs of breasts, indicating her ability to suckle the whole of creation. Cybele is also the name of a friend I made at my kids' pre-school during the early years of mothering. In conversations, Cybele, profoundly deaf from birth, would use gestures like a mime, to make sure I was following what she said.

"A Soul So Watched" is for my family. The epigraph is from Sylvia Plath's "The Moon and the Yew Tree."

On page 38, the parenthetical interjection "I apologize / for writing this" I came upon in a poem by Osip Mandelstam, during the writing of this section of my book. It spoke to how strongly I wanted to stop the writing, and apologize—make a hole in the a poem's protective fourth wall.

The italicized lines on page 45 are from "Suicide: Psychache and Alienation" (*Psychiatric Times*, Nov. 8, 2011, by Michael Sperber, MD).

The last line of page 45 quotes David Hume.

The second-to-last sentence of the final section of "A Soul So Watched" paraphrases the Venerable Bede, as quoted in Marguerite Yourcenar's *That Mighty Sculptor, Time.*

"Tilted Stones" is for Will and Finn.

The italicized lines in "Vanitas" reference William James's essay "Is Life Worth Living?"

The description "silver and exact" is from Plath's "Mirror."

In "Why Ever Winter" the phrase "loveless dust" is Yeats.

"Pastoral" is for Tom Thompson.

Acknowledgments

I'm grateful to the editors and staff of the following journals and periodicals, where these poems have appeared:

Bomb, Columbia, Cortland Review, La Petite Zine, Literary Imagination, The Literary Review, Ploughshares, and *TriQuarterly.*

Many thanks to Martha Rhodes and Ryan Murphy, and all at Four Way Books, first of all for selecting my manuscript, then for the creative energy they've poured into bringing the book to publication. I was also extremely fortunate to work with Bridget Bell on the book's final edits and corrections; her sensitivity to the smallest details of syntax, punctuation, tone and typography—and her voice at the other end of the line—were infinitely calming at the most nerve-wracking stage of the process.

I owe a vast debt of gratitude to many whose art, and love, and friendship, and nurturing, and wisdom, and brilliance, and faith in my work have sustained me through the writing of this book, as well as through the years of silence that preceded it. Among them: Catherine Barnett, Christina Davis, Regan Good, Julia Guez, Saskia Hamilton, Judy Jensen, Rebecca Kinzie-Bastian, James Longenbach, Michelle Meier, Fiona Wilson, and Rachel Zucker.

And to Constance Stewart, whose name reflects her patient care; who helped me make my way slowly through the tangle of thorns.

And to my awesome parents, Carla Brelos Field and John H. Field; and the formidable "sistren": Gaby, Gill, Jenny; and all of our children, each of whom has changed our lives and made us grow.

Above all, to Tom, Will, and Finn: You inspire and keep me. You show me what love is.

Miranda Field received a Katherine Bakeless Nason Literary Publication Award for her first book, *Swallow* (Houghton Mifflin, 2002). Born and raised in North London, UK, she lives and works in Manhattan, where she teaches in the Creative Writing programs at New York University, Eugene Lang College, and Barnard College.

Publication of this book was made possible by grants and donations. We are also grateful to those individuals who participated in our 2016 Build a Book Program. They are:

Anonymous (8), Evan Archer, Sally Ball, Jan Bender-Zanoni, Zeke Berman, Kristina Bicher, Carol Blum, Lee Briccetti, Deirdre Brill, Anthony Cappo, Carla & Steven Carlson, Maxwell Dana, Machi Davis, Monica Ferrell, Martha Webster & Robert Fuentes, Dorothy Goldman, Lauri Grossman, Steven Haas, Mary Heilner, Henry Israeli, Christopher Kempf, David Lee, Jen Levitt, Howard Levy, Owen Lewis, Paul Lisicky, Katie Longofono, Cynthia Lowen, Louise Mathias, Nathan McClain, Gregory McDonald, Britt Melewski, Kamilah Aisha Moon, Carolyn Murdoch, Tracey Orick, Zachary Pace, Gregory Pardlo, Allyson Paty, Marcia & Chris Pelletiere, Eileen Pollack, Barbara Preminger, Kevin Prufer, Peter & Jill Schireson, Roni & Richard Schotter, Soraya Shalforoosh, Peggy Shinner, James Snyder & Krista Fragos, Megan Staffel, Marjorie & Lew Tesser, Susan Walton, Calvin Wei, Abigail Wender, Allison Benis White, and Monica Youn.